BEWARE OF FLOODS

MATT REHER   APRIL FERRY

TABLE OF CONTENTS

Introduction 4

A Natural Disaster 6

Flood Zones 7

Common Kinds of Floods

   1. River Flooding (Fluvial) 8

   2. Surface or Urban Flooding (Pluvial) 12

   3. Coastal Flooding (Surge) 14

Flood Safety 16

Impacts of Flooding 18

Reducing the Impacts of Flooding 22

Collecting Flood Data 26

Conclusion 28

Index

INTRODUCTION

One of the worst floods in America happened on August 29, 2005. This flood happened in the city of New Orleans. It was caused by Hurricane Katrina. People were trapped in their homes and had to climb onto their roofs for safety. About 80% of the city was underwater for weeks. Many people lost everything they owned, and more than 1,000 people died.

A NATURAL DISASTER

Flooding happens when there is too much water in one place and there's no place for the water to go. Floods can happen in all 50 states. Floods are one of the most common disasters.

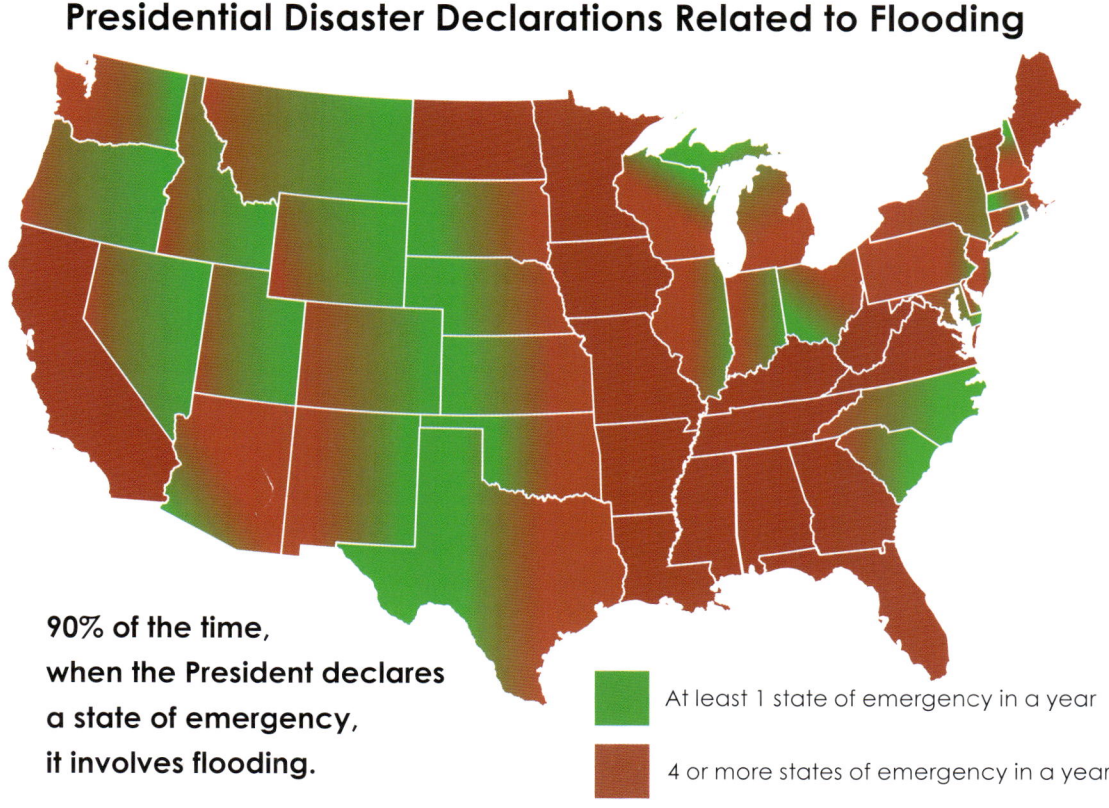

Presidential Disaster Declarations Related to Flooding

90% of the time, when the President declares a state of emergency, it involves flooding.

■ At least 1 state of emergency in a year
■ 4 or more states of emergency in a year

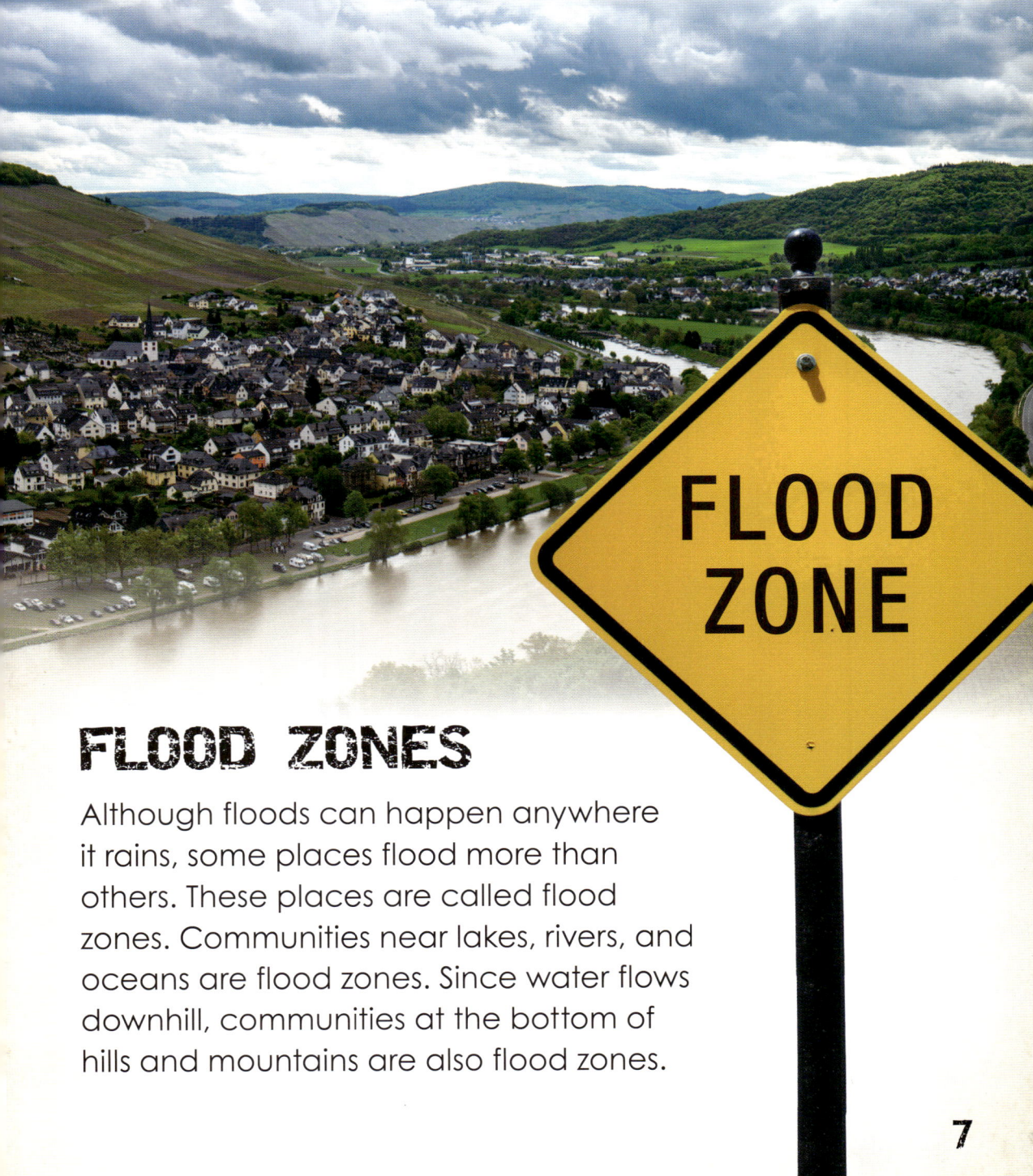

FLOOD ZONES

Although floods can happen anywhere it rains, some places flood more than others. These places are called flood zones. Communities near lakes, rivers, and oceans are flood zones. Since water flows downhill, communities at the bottom of hills and mountains are also flood zones.

COMMON KINDS OF FLOODS
1. River Flooding (Fluvial)

The most common kind of flooding is river flooding. River flooding happens when too much rain adds too much water to rivers and lakes. This extra water overflows, or spills out, causing a flood. Water from melting snow can also cause river floods. Every year in the United States, there are more than 100 river floods.

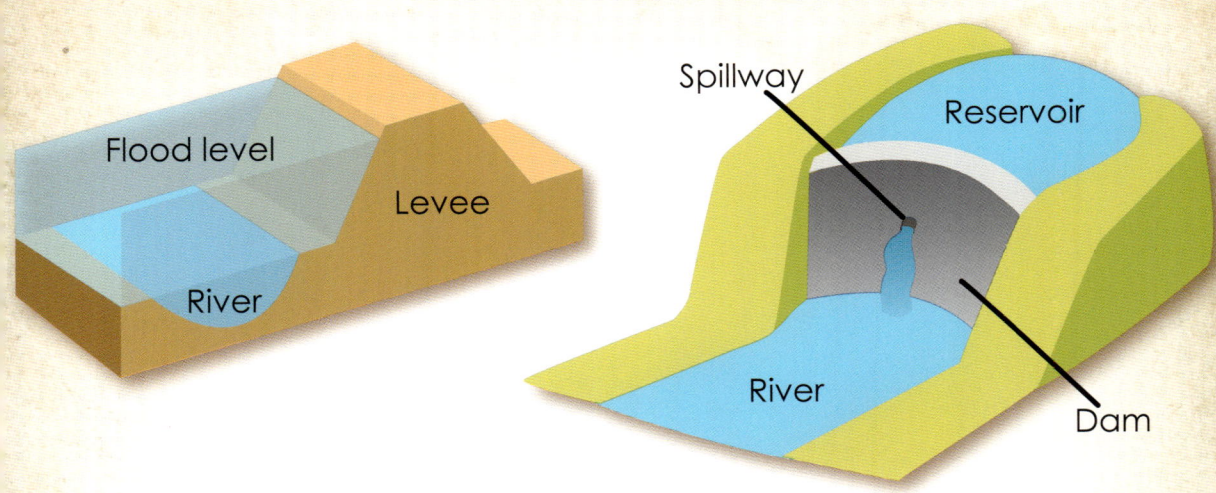

Cities build walls to try to keep water out of flood zones. These walls are called dams or levees. New Orleans has levees along the Mississippi River and Lake Pontchartrain. Levees and dams don't always work. During Hurricane Katrina, the levees broke. About 250 billion gallons of water flooded into neighborhoods.

The most dangerous kind of river flooding is a flash flood. Flash floods are caused by heavy rain, and they usually happen very quickly—within 3 hours of the storm. Flash floods kill about 200 people every year. Flash flood water moves quickly, so people don't have a lot of time to get to safety.

Flash flood water may not be very deep, but it's still dangerous. Just two feet of water is enough water to move a school bus. In fact, most flash flood deaths happen when people try to drive their cars through shallow flood water.

2. Surface or Urban Flooding (Pluvial)

When it rains, water usually soaks into the ground and gets used by plants. But, in big cities, the ground is often used for highways and parking lots, so most of the ground is covered with concrete. Unlike dirt, concrete doesn't soak up water. When the rain water gets stuck on top of the concrete, surface floods happen.

Many big cities use sewer systems of drains and pipes to carry water away. But, when there's too much rain, the pipes can't carry the water away fast enough, and cities end up with surface flooding. Surface floods aren't very dangerous. The water moves slowly, but it does make it hard for people to walk or drive through the city.

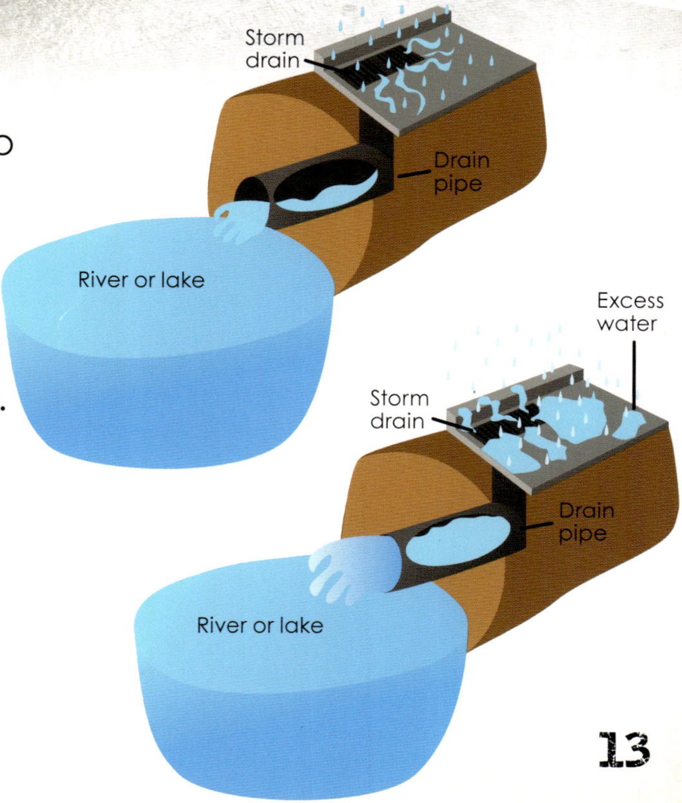

3. Coastal Flooding (Surge)

Coastal flooding happens in communities nearest to an ocean or lake. In the United States, about 39% of people live near oceans or lakes. Coastal flooding is caused by large waves of water moving toward land and flooding the coast.

NUMBER OF PEOPLE LIVING HERE: 124,733,542

Some of the largest waves are caused by powerful hurricane winds. These waves are called storm surges. New Orleans had many storm surges during Hurricane Katrina, but the largest storm surges happened in the town of Pass Christian, Mississippi. They were more than 27 feet tall.

FLOOD SAFETY

People who live in flood zones should keep some things in their homes in case of a flood. This includes extra food and water, batteries, flashlights, and first aid supplies like bandages, scissors, and ice packs.

There are many ways to stay safe during a flood. First of all, people should never try to drive during a flood. People should stay inside, go to the highest floor of the house, and stay away from electronics. It's also possible that a community will be asked to evacuate, or leave their homes, before a flood comes.

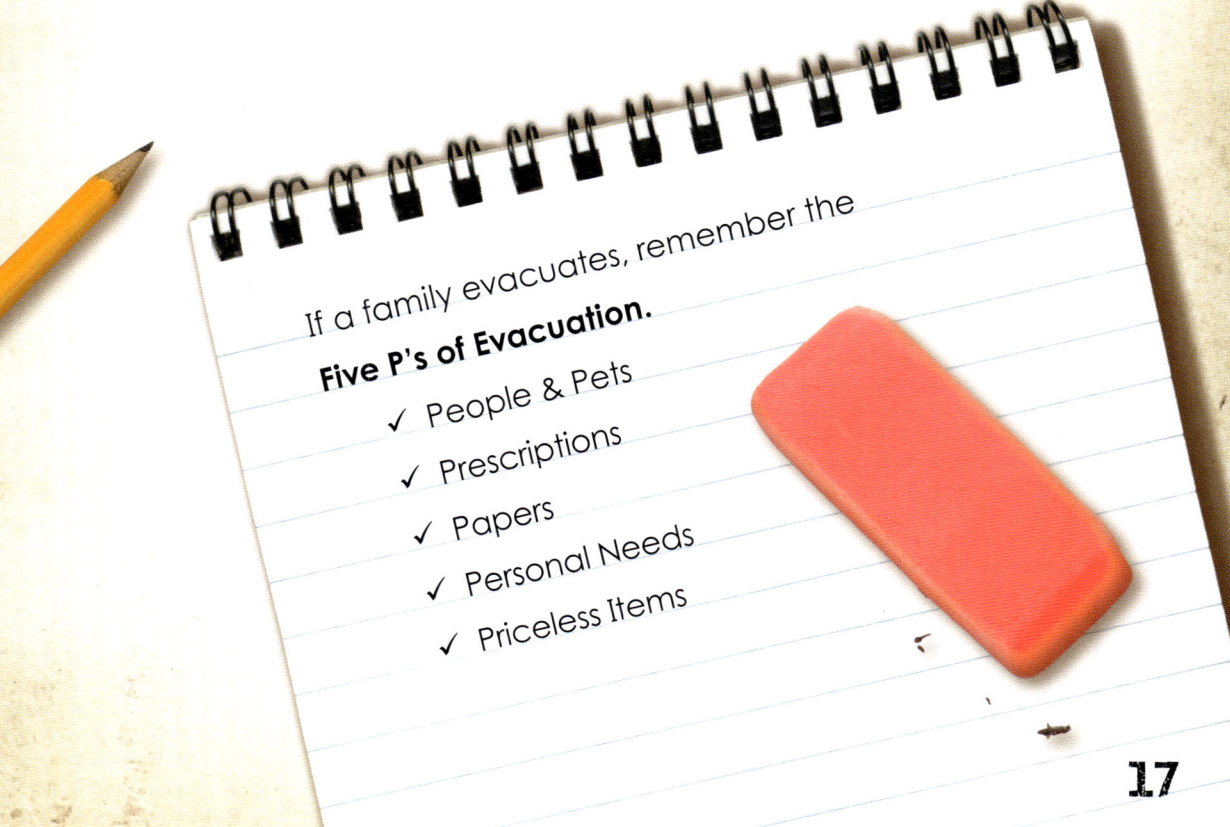

If a family evacuates, remember the
Five P's of Evacuation.
- ✓ People & Pets
- ✓ Prescriptions
- ✓ Papers
- ✓ Personal Needs
- ✓ Priceless Items

IMPACTS OF FLOODING

Fixing the damage caused by flooding costs lots of money. Just one foot of flood water in a home could cost the homeowner more than $50,000. Hurricane Katrina caused more than $20 billion in flood damage to the city of New Orleans.

Flood water can be harmful to the health of people and animals. The water might carry many dangerous things in it like oil, trash, and chemicals. These things could make people and animals very sick.

When a community floods often, people start to move away and find new places to live. This is called population displacement. The number of people living in New Orleans before the flooding was 484,674 people. Months later, there were only 254,504 people living there.

Flooding is harmful to the environment. Flooding on the coasts breaks up the land. Some parts of the land wash away into the ocean. This is called erosion. Erosion changes the way the land looks over time.

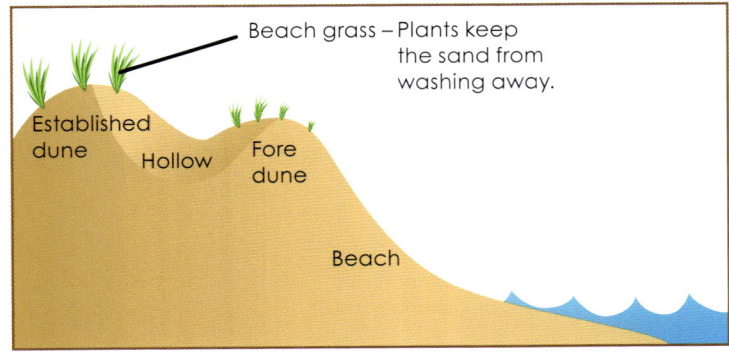

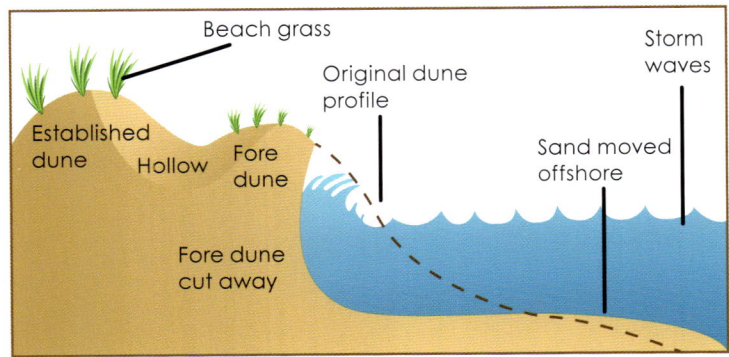

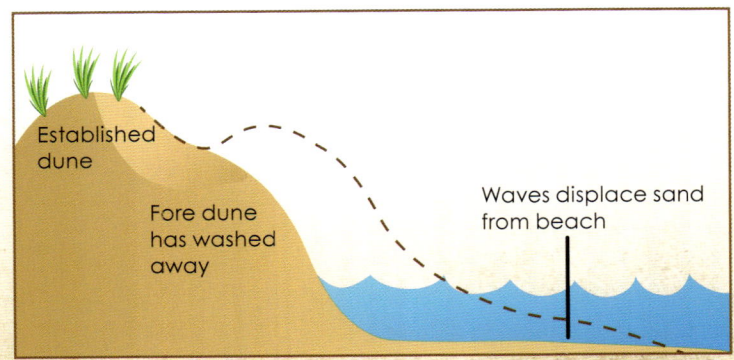

REDUCING THE IMPACTS OF FLOODS

People who make machines to solve problems are called engineers. Many engineers are working on ways to make flooding less dangerous. Engineers are building seawalls. There are three kinds of seawalls: vertical, curved, and mound. These walls can be expensive to build, but each wall works to keep people and land safe from flooding.

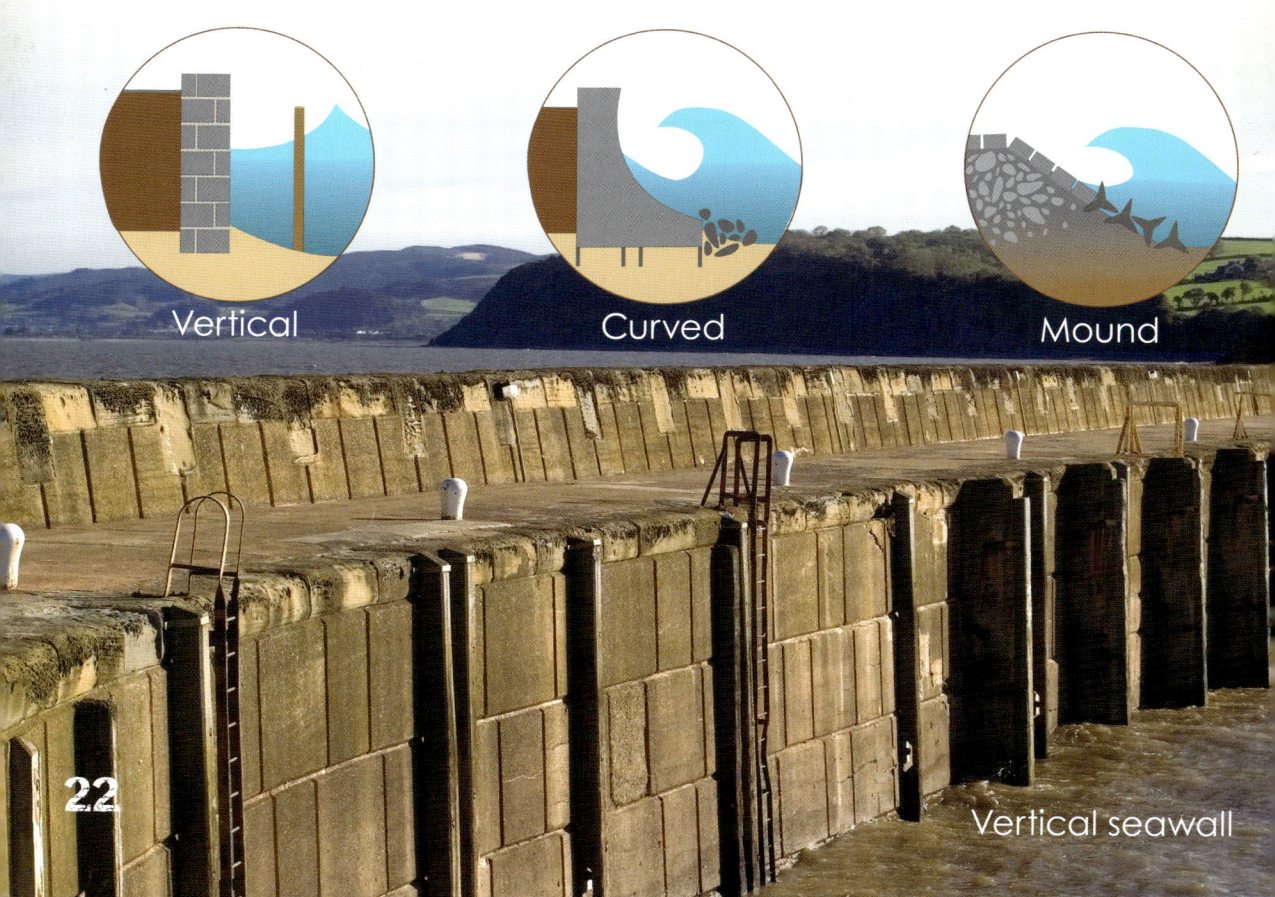

Vertical

Curved

Mound

Vertical seawall

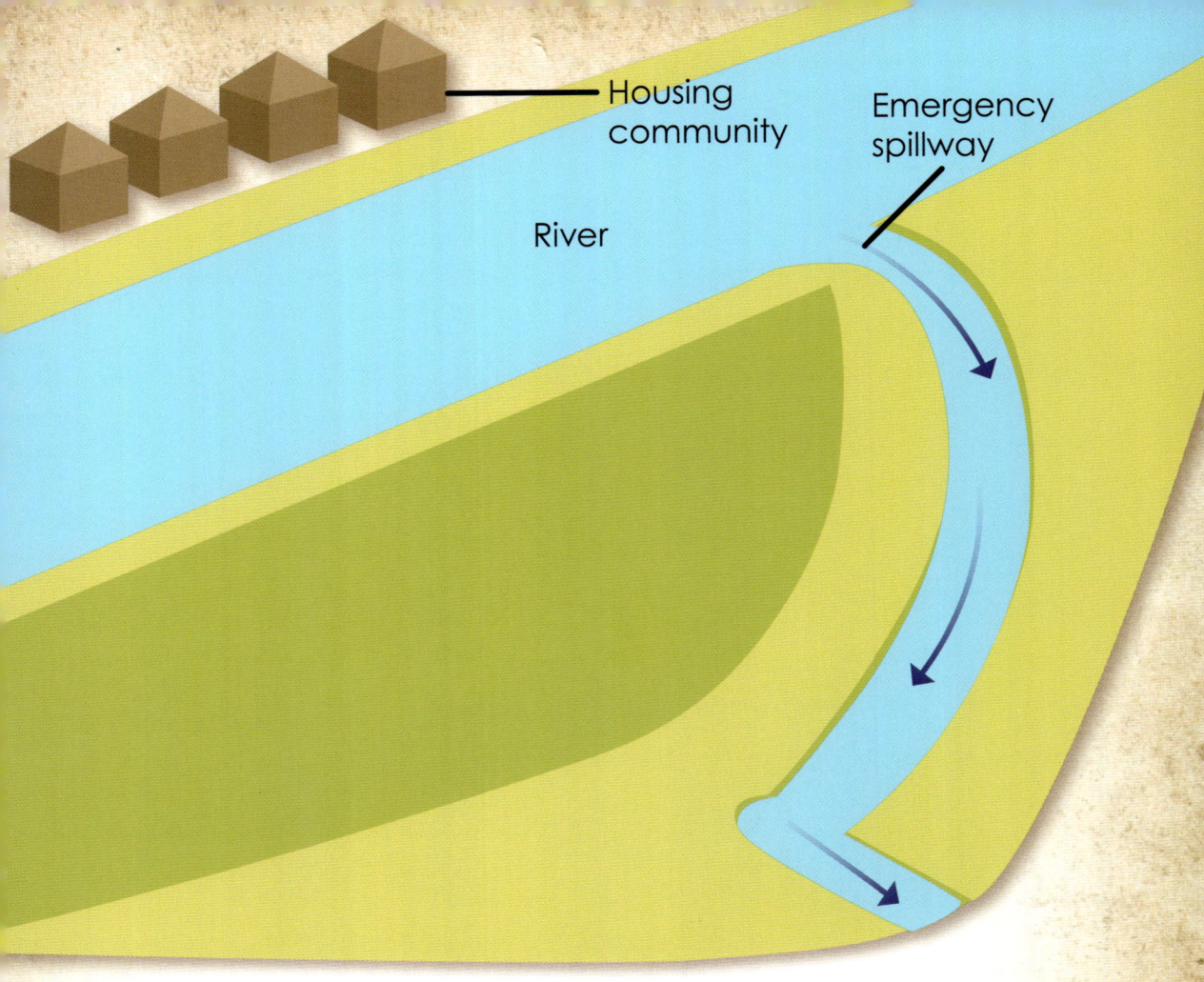

Engineers are also building spillways. A spillway is a path for flood water. Some spillways are built near rivers. If the river water gets high, engineers open the spillway. Water flows from the river into the spillway. The spillway moves the water away from communities.

Wetlands are helpful during a flood. Flood water slows down when it crashes into the wetland plants and trees. The many plants in the wetlands also stop the land from washing away into the ocean. This is one reason scientists are working to save the wetlands.

In areas that flood often, people are building their homes higher off the ground. Engineers are also designing homes to be safer by placing electrical sockets higher up on walls. Some engineers are designing homes that can float in case of a flood.

COLLECTING FLOOD DATA

To prepare for the dangers of flooding in the future, scientists study floods. They record, or write down, the exact place, date, and time of the flooding. They also study the cause of the flood.

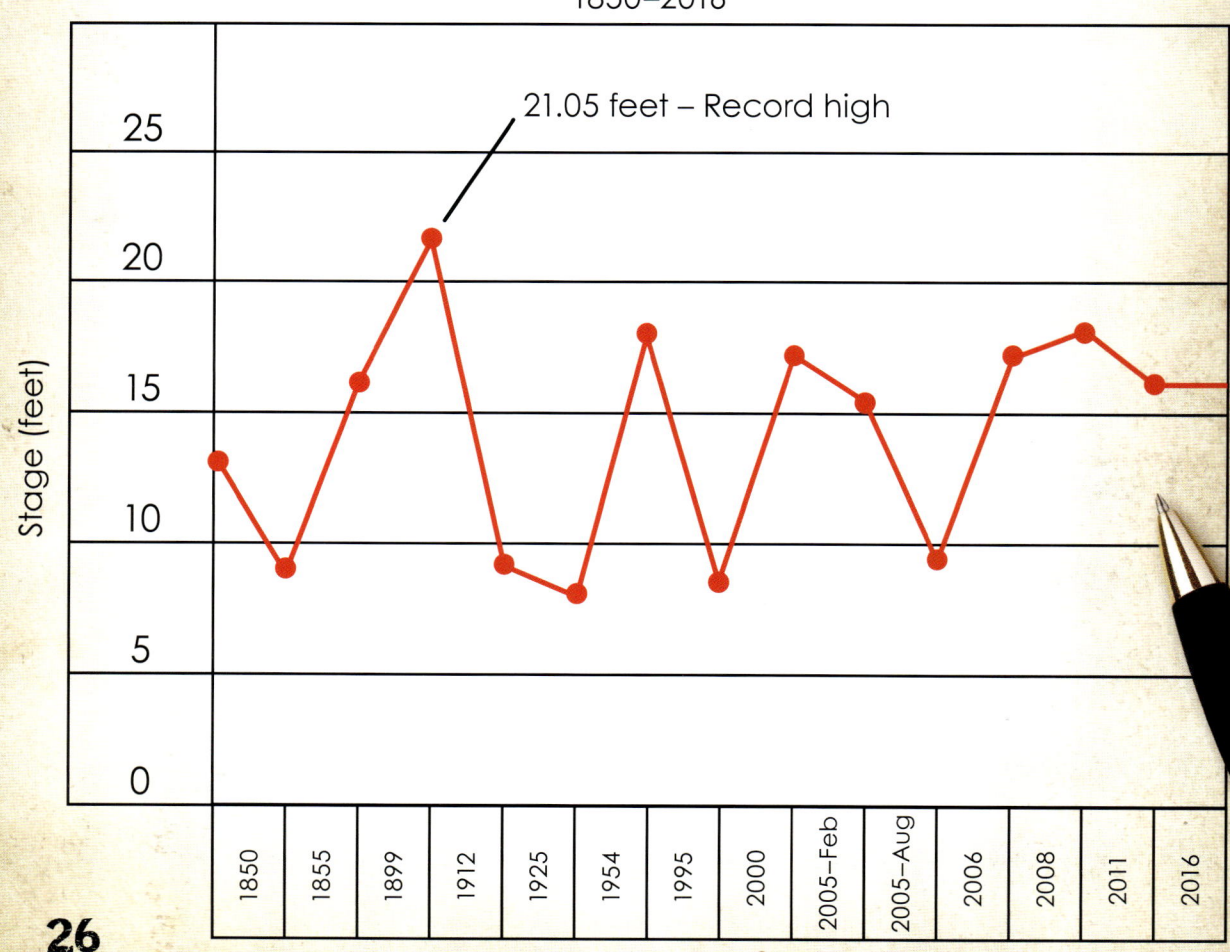

Historic Floods in New Orleans
1850–2016

The flood level is the most important information. It tells the scientists exactly how high the floodwater got. Sometimes, scientists are able to see the flood level by looking at the strandline. A strandline is a line left on a building by the water and dirt from the flood.

CONCLUSION

The city of New Orleans wasn't prepared for such a huge flood. Hurricane Katrina taught the city and the country how important it is to be prepared. Engineers rebuilt the levees in New Orleans to be stronger and taller, but the levees still aren't strong enough to handle the floods from the biggest hurricanes and storm surges. It's important that scientists continue to study floods and their dangers.